# The Code

# For

# Love

**A Man's Guide to Understanding Women**

**John McRae**

# Acknowledgements

I wish to give a very special thank you to God Almighty, for if it had not been for his love, this book would never have been published.

He has shown the world a new gift for which I am most grateful.

# Forward

A new era, a new mindset, a new sense of peace. Better relationships, a better way to love. Aligning one's self to be calm and not going overboard. Going through issues that will or could blow over anyway. Jumping down her throat which in the end will be a matter so simple! Thrown pots and pans, thrown dishes; broken, abusive circumstances and over egotism. The list goes on and on.

This book will be the first step for all men to realize, why am I really with her? How can I make it right? As you read this book, I want you to realize the Godsend.

This book is based on the truth.  A matter that was by mistake revealed to me to be something more than one expected to be very effective.

As I research and analyzed situations, I was implored to tell the world of this finding by a medical doctor, a couple of ministers, educators, professionals, over and over again.  Males and females alike waited for the moment to arrive when they would see the book that could change lives.  Yes this is real!

When you finish reading this book, I would like you to also thank the Lord for this information,

Lastly, I want people to put aside their thoughts of sacrilegious idiom for really there is none in this book.  For years many people have used colloquial terms in statements, such as, an ass, which is actually written in the Bible.

But when used incorrectly, the word, "ass" is considered profanity. The term "pussy" is used, and I apologize in advance to anyone who deems this term to be derogatory.

You will be reading a story that was shared in private between me and my best friend.

There are no overboard sexual drafts, just true stories and statements used and shared with you. I promise, if you use your intellect to its full advantage, you will understand this book.

Moving forward I plan to take this knowledge to an even higher level. One method will be to continue to use physicians, psychologists and attorneys to propel this exercise to an ongoing perfection.

# Introduction:

Since the beginning of time, males have not been able to understand women. Divorce rates have doubled, and it is said that 60 percent of all marriages end in divorce. This is a substantial increase of 10% over the past 20 years.

But why? Why can't men understand women? Why is it so apparent that all men say the same things?

Just about every man I have encounter will say, "My wife is crazy." "I don't understand why she gets on my nerves!" And when the subject is introduced to another gentleman, he says that his girl is the same way.

Now, it was always said that a man cannot break the secret. I believe I have. Yes, the secret is out, and I have been evaluating this for over two years.

So get ready. I am going to show you how to get along with your mate, and have the love of your life loving you more and more each day.

By the time you complete this book you are going to be the man you always wanted to be: A king, a man, and very well respected. Perhaps your thoughts of divorce or breakup will cease.

The time has come so get ready. It's time to just get the p.

# Table of Contents

# Chapter I

## <u>Just get the P*ssy</u>

Well, the title of this chapter, I'm sure, has you amused. However, I'm not talking about the feline species. I am talking about a major part of the female genitalia, the vagina.

The vagina--mans most sacred prize. The best invention since the dawn of human life. The single item a man will pay thousands of dollars for.

Ask any man, take a pick, any man you want, choose one or the other: A new car for the rest of your life, or all the excellent pussy you want, when you want it, and how you want it.

Take your pick, one or the other!  Well, personally I will take the pussy.

Why:  For one reason, it is very hard to come by.  You may search long for it, and when you get it, you don't want to lose it.

Secondly, it feels better than a car. You know what I mean.  A car isn't human, and you could walk any day of the week if you need to do so.

Cars give you trouble; they will lock you up in traffic, etc.  You may get horny, yet a car will not relieve you.  Oh, you think that you can masturbate and be happy?  Ok there is only one problem.  For a man, that issue is very limited.

For one, after having relieved his inside manhood, a man will feel very lonely, because he has lost a lot of the living sperm cells in his body.  And for another, no matter what, a man longs for that sweet soft body, to caress, to love in sickness or in health and for companionship.

Shortly after sex, while you're tired, relaxing, waiting for another moment of great sex, you can be assured, of nothing else: a good bout is about to happen.

The arguments follow and surely, there will be no understanding from both parties. It's like, to hell with the sex thing.

Well men I'm here to tell you: Just get the p. Yes, I said it, and you know it. Men, what is the only thing you really want in life? You could care less about curtains, the color of the flowers, the new carpeting, linen thread counts, etc.

Think about it! You're right! PUSSY!!!!!! Admit it, you know I'm right. You've worked hard all day. Your mind has been taxed. Bills are due, and as a man you are going to pay them.

Your wife needs things, and you are going to take care of them to the best of your ability. Why? Because, of a vagina.

On an average day, men think about it from the time he sees his wife until the end of the day. Ladies may think that we are saying good morning, but in actuality we are saying, "Good morning. I want sex." And we are mature enough to be kind. From the moment we see a female's face; we think sex, sex, sex.

What happens in our lives, though, if we have an argument? She would either have said, or did something that absolutely made no sense at all, and it entirely pissed you off to the point that you will pack up and move out, just to have peace of mind.

But I am here to tell you: Just get the p. Calm down, go through it, and keep saying to yourself: Just get the p, just get the p, and just get the p, over and over again.

Go into another room, or just leave for a few minutes, but keep saying, "Just get the p." When you come back, things will be calmer, and then the panties will come off. In essence, the victory is yours.

# CHAPTER 2

## <u>How it Started</u>.

My theory started from a counseling session. I was ready to get rid of my wife. I just couldn't take it anymore. The therapist mentioned in the meeting that his girl was the same as my wife. Having been married for many years, I laughed to myself. No way are you going to be married for that many years, and they are alike. The session ended and I conceded to the concepts that were discussed.

But how is his girl like mine? I thought about it for a couple of days, and it hit me. They both have a vagina. Maybe he did not know what I was thinking, then reality set in: Just get the p.

So I stopped trying to understand her.  Women are hard to understand.  I put it in my mind to stop arguing with her because arguing will only delay my chance to get the p.  And the last thing a man needs is to not know where he is going to have his next fix: some sex, the joyful delight.   It is the only thing we live for.  It's all we have.

It is like going to the store and not having ice-cream.  Like cornflakes without the milk; like a peanut butter sandwich without the jelly.  You know what I mean.  It is like a bicycle tire, without the bicycle.  The list goes on and on.

Well, I'm sure that by now you are thinking, it sounds good, but does it really work?"  Check this out.

I told this to my mechanic who is my friend. He is a great mechanic, and he has a very pretty girlfriend.  He tried the method first.

At times he thought, "Just get the p, just get the p. He took it easy with her, and things were going well.

Then, one day he called me and was very upset. I could hear his voice through the phone he was about to cry. I asked him what was wrong? He said, "My girl had another man at the house." At first I thought, "Dam, that's a bad thing." But then it hit me. Then I told him,     "Just get the p. He was very surprised at what I said.

What?" said he? I then repeated, "Just get the p." He then said, "That is just what I'm going to do!" Shortly thereafter, their relationship became closer, better than before. We both continued to use this method, and one day she confirmed to us of how effectively it works.

Recently, at a Super Bowl Party, a few of the ladies went out to smoke cigarettes and to chat.

She stayed back with us, and asked me, "What do you and my man say to each other? You both treat your ladies with so much respect and calmness. What do you say to my man!"

Caught off guard I said, "Well we both tell each other to JUST GIVE THE LOVE!" She was pleased at my response. She then joined the other ladies outdoors and to smoke along with them. When she left out the door, we had the most gut—wrenching, jaw dropping, eyes crying laugh for about a good five minutes. I couldn't tell her the full truth (Just get the Pussy). But it was at that moment that we knew we were on to something.

Another story he told me was even funnier.

He said that he was telling his lady, to not back the car out the way she was backing it out because she would wreck the car. He told her to correct it and try to back out again.

Because she didn't listen, she did it her way and knocked the bumper off the car.

He didn't yell at her, for in his mind there was no reason to fuss. He just picked up the bumper, put it in the trunk of the car, and drove off and fixed it.

The next week he came back. You know what happened (need I need to say more?) She was so sorry, and pleased that he didn't get upset.

As time went by we thought of a new more pleasurable ways to say it. So we came up with a new code: JUST GET THE P, JUST GET THE P.

# CHAPTER 3

## <u>Male Erectile Dysfunction</u>

This chapter will deal with a function of men that will be somewhat disheartening, that being, Erectile Dysfunction (ED)

Now, I am not an expert physician on this subject by any means.  But I am sure , that what you will read is accurate.  In fact, it has been proven.

It is my analogy that some erectile dysfunction is cause by a man being very wise.  Most females may think that a man does not use his brain, but only his penis to think.

I have found that now being 51 years old, this may be somewhat very true.

Most men with ED are older and very wise men. I feel the reason for this problem is because we have come too far with our mate. We are at a point where we just deal with situations, and just fall into a hidden kind of depression.

The reason I can say this is because of street smarts, and of an older gentleman who I have taught the just get the p method.

He asked me "What if I can't do it?" And I explained to him that even though you may have made up with her, you are still scared of the future. You're more worried about, "I'm going to drop this load and she is going to start up again."

But now you won't care, because every time you get into an argument, you will say over and over to yourself in your mind, just get the p, just get the p, and just get the p.

For example: she says you are the dumbest mother @#$% I ever knew.

You are thinking as she says it, just get the p, just get the p. You go into another room, or leave the house. And as you leave she is behind you shouting, "I hate you, I never loved you, you piece of #$%$! Go, go!"

All along you are saying to yourself, "Just get the p, just get the p.

Now in most relationships the makeup period comes next. Usually the women will be saddened about all she said, and she will want to give you something to show you how remorseful she is.

In fact, maybe she will be horny from the fight. And sometimes the guy will hold off from sex, or try to do it, but just can't get it up.  In reality that is all he wanted from the start.

So now after all that talk she did, she removes her undergarments.  In turn, you just get the p.

Now you have seen the picture of a cat.  But trust me.  It may look mean. But it's not. It's just a picture.  You have to get it into your mind another idea.

When a man penetrates his female's vagina, it feels very good to him.  It will be most satisfying for you and for her also,  when she is happy knowing, that you are still are her man.

Most of the time after an argument, the lady is somewhere crying, and somewhere hoping that you forgive her.  Yeah, you will forgive her alright. But in your mind you are thinking, hell something else is going to happen.  Eventually, she will curse you out again, piss you off, and drive you crazy.

And all you should think about is, just get the p!!!!

Just get the p!!!!!

Getting back to the older gentlemen I spoke of earlier.

The next time I saw the older guy; he said, "Hey man Ha Ha Ha Ha Ha!" Then I said, "Ha Ha Ha?" He said, "Yeah, Ha Ha Ha Ha Ha!!!!" Then, we both cracked up laughing.

# Chapter 4

## <u>Real Stories of Just Get the P</u>

Like the story of the highway patrol, here are some stories of how effective just get the p is.

I know you heard the story of the car bumper. Let's talk for a minute about a few more just get the p stories.

A co-worker of mine was doing the just get the P method very well. Then one day he came to me and said, "I tried and I tried but, I had to move out, and I have since gotten my own apartment."

Now, I, not being ignorant to the situation, I asked him, "Did you just get the p?" He said he hadn't but he moved out instead.

Ok, two weeks passed by. I believed that since he was still married, he could make up with his wife and "get a little" at any time. Again, I asked him, "Did you just get the p yet?" He said he did not and that the party was over and that life was good.

Well, yes, life is good. I thought to myself, "Sure it is." Hummm...??

Ok, two more weeks passed, and I asked him again, in a more direct matter of voice, "DID YOU JUST GET THE P?!!!" His response to me was that every key doesn't fit the same hole, and for me to remember that statement.

Well, two more weeks passed and he came to me and said that he had moved back home with his wife, and that they had chose to reconciliate.

When he told me, I didn't burst out in laughter; however, I was somewhat upset.

Then I told him that he could have saved a whole bunch of time and money, if he had just thought the magic words:

"JUST GET THE P, JUST GET THE P!"

As gentlemen, we have the tendency to let our head brain, have power over our penis brain. Don't do it! If, you mess with the penis' vagina, it will mess you up. So don't be a big shot. Don't be so big with your chest stuck out. Get some, keep getting some, love it, and enjoy it.

Another story of mine--and I have plenty of them to share—goes like this. I was taking to another old gentleman who I taught the just get the p method. At first when you tell a man about it, they start laughing, primarily because it was a thought that has been on our minds, but we never applied it.

Because of his age, and having been married for some 25 years, I asked him a few questions which follow:

What happens when you have feelings for other women and you haven't done "it" in a while? He quickly responded with the meanest look in his eyes and said,

"JUST STICK WITH THE PLAN,!!!!!!------

JUST STICK WITH THE PLAN!!!!!!!!!"

This told me, that after 20 some odd years of marriage, he had found the remedy to a long lasting, and more peaceful relationship.  And, he would have probably never thought of cheating, in the first place.

Another true story, and I do have many more is, one day I called my love on her cell phone. Among other things we talked about, we talked about finances.  In the middle of the conversation

she asked, "WHEN ARE YOU GOING TO TAKE ME

OUT?"

Now gentlemen, can you imagine how upset I

was?  Here I am trying to figure out, how to keep

our heads above water, and all she wanted to know

is when we were going out.

I had to get off the phone, because I was about

to blow a gasket.  So rather than go berserk, I

politely hung up.  Mad as hell, I kept saying to

myself, "just get the p, just get the p."  But it wasn't

enough.  I had to think quickly, so I called my

mechanic friend.  I asked him to just say it to me.  I

needed to hear it, please tell me.  He exclaimed over

and over again with authority:

"JUST GET THE P, MAN JUST GET THE P.!!!!

THERE IS NOTHING ELSE YOU CAN DO!! , JUST GET

THE P!  NO OTHER HELP, JUST GET IT, AND GET IT! AND GET IT, JUST GET THE P!

What relief that was.  It was soothing to my ears.  Days passed, finances were discussed with maturity, no arguments, no foul language.  Just get the p had won again.

One must realize problems are going to happen.  Be calm, be a man, stand firm.  And keep saying the magic phrase.  It's the law.  If you break the law,  you will suffer one way or another.

This method is not fool proof, but it will save you some time and money.  There have been instances of where I wanted to go completely off the planet.  But I said to myself, "To hell with it, just get the p."  There was a time, when I wanted to win an argument.  With all my might, I thought that she will not win this argument.  I was going to give it to her, with all the full intensity of my being.

But before I started the argument, she came to me and reasoned with the situation.

After you do this exercise so often, it may become second nature. So the problem was fixed, whatever it was, with calmness. Little did she know, what I was thinking all along at times, just get the p.

# Chapter 5

## <u>Reasons to get the P.</u>

Let's face it. By now we have to understand that there is no reason not to get the p. But just in case you didn't get the picture, here are some reasons that may help you.

If your lady wrecks the car, and didn't pay the automobile insurance, JUST GET THE P.

If she burns the dinner, JUST GET THE P.

When you come home from a hard day's work and the house is filthy. Clean it yourself and JUST GET THE P.

When she drinks too much and says something totally stupid, JUST GET THE P.

When the rent is due, and she spent the money to buy shoes, don't get mad, calm down and JUST GET THE P.

As you both are ready to go out and she is late as hell to get dressed, bite your tongue, remain calm, and JUST GET THE P.

When you finish this book, and for some reason, she still gets on your nerves--believe me she will--JUST GET THE P.

Finally, this should have been the #1 reason: No matter, no matter what, JUST GET THE P!!!!

## THE END

# Author's note

There you have it, one of the best books ever written. Why? It was not planned. Was it long overdue? Yes, I believe it was , and very much so.

When I set out to do this book I was always taught to put God first in all that we do.

When people asked me when will the book be published, would tell them that it would be published in God's time.

You may ask; how can I use God, and say that He was helping me? I am a Christian. I ask our Heavenly Father daily to forgive us of our trespasses as we forgive those who trespass against us.

I asked God, how can I do this?  And I remembered Moses, who God had led to free the slaves.  They walked through the desert with no food.  Moses was able to open the Red Sea for passage into the Promised Land.

Then people would ask, how can I use such a word as pussy?  I would explain that it is a cat.  But if a man is crying about his relationship to another man, what would be the best way to convince him of what to do about his relationship?  For example, just have sex? Just get the vagina? Just do the cat? Or will he easier understand that you are serious when you say to him just get the pussy or P.

Samson defeated an army with a jawbone of an ass.  I have saved relationships with the use of one word.

Let's examine some of the greatest inventions in the world today.

The Airplane. When it was invented, the plane lifted off the ground and flew several feet. But it crashed, and then was perfected to fly longer distances, and to higher heights. Today, we have airplanes which fly around the world.

Another invention is the automobile. It started out as a good product, and had some problems here and there. But as time goes on, there are major improvements being made. Today, we have cruise control, global position sensors, mapping, and all sorts of sensors and great gadgets within them.

So why can't we use this as a stepping stone. The sky's the limit.

Imagine when you walk your daughter down the aisle at her wedding, and the confidence that you as a father will have, thinking maybe she will have a better chance for life happiness, because of this book.

If I may, let me tell you a short story. I would go to my medical doctor. And on occasion I would mention that my blood pressure might be up because of arguing with my wife. He tried to help me, but not too much availed.

One day I came in and he asked me, how we were doing in our marriage? Caught off guard again, I had to tell him the truth. I told him that I have come up with a new saying to help me. He asked what it was. I told him, "I just tell myself to just get the pussy." He laughed and told me that I was on to something. I asked if I should write a book and he said yes. He still to this day encourages and teaches me to follow up on more research, and not to quit.

I want to further emphasize that this prose is not a full proof. You still must put in the work. But

I'll guarantee this much.  It will be a lot easier for men to follow this method, than to go it alone.

Continue to pray to your Higher Power, and thank your woman once in a while for being in your life.  Cherish the ground she walks on.  Why? Cause you love her, and she has the piece!!

John McRae

www.ingramcontent.com/pod-product-compliance
Lightning Source LLC
Chambersburg PA
CBHW070243290526
45789CB00004B/1745